PROFESSOR PETER COOPER is Professor of Psychology at the University of Reading and Honorary NHS Consultant Clinical Psychologist. He has worked for many years in the field of eating disorders, specializing in bulimia nervosa and binge-eating. His original book on bulimia nervosa founded the *Overcoming* series in 1993 and continues to help many thousands of people in the USA, the UK and Europe. The aim of the series is to help people with a wide range of common problems and disorders to take control of their own recovery programme using the latest techniques of cognitive behavioural therapy. Each book, with its specially tailored programme, is devised by a practising clinician. Many books in the *Overcoming* series are now recommended by the UK Department of Health under the Books on Prescription scheme. Following a self-help programme is recommended as a possible first step for those suffering from bulimia nervosa by the National Institute for Health and Clinical Excellence (NICE).

Other titles in the *Overcoming* series:

3-part self-help courses

Overcoming Anxiety Self-Help Course
Overcoming Low Self-Esteem Self-Help Course
Overcoming Panic and Agoraphobia Self-Help Course
Overcoming Social Anxiety and Shyness Self-Help Course

Single-volume books

Overcoming Anger and Irritability
Overcoming Anorexia Nervosa
Overcoming Anxiety
Bulimia Nervosa and Binge-Eating
Overcoming Childhood Trauma
Overcoming Chronic Fatigue
Overcoming Chronic Pain
Overcoming Compulsive Gambling
Overcoming Depression
Overcoming Insomnia and Sleep Problems
Overcoming Low Self-Esteem
Overcoming Mood Swings
Overcoming Obsessive Compulsive Disorder
Overcoming Panic
Overcoming Paranoid and Suspicious Thoughts
Overcoming Problem Drinking
Overcoming Relationship Problems
Overcoming Sexual Problems
Overcoming Social Anxiety and Shyness
Overcoming Traumatic Stress
Overcoming Weight Problems
Overcoming Your Child's Fears and Worries
Overcoming Your Smoking Habit

OVERCOMING BULIMIA AND BINGE-EATING SELF-HELP COURSE

A 3-part programme based on Cognitive Behavioural Techniques

Part Three: Problem Solving, How to Stop Dieting and How to Change Your Mind

Peter J. Cooper

ROBINSON
London

Constable & Robinson Ltd
3 The Lanchesters
162 Fulham Palace Road
London W6 9ER
www.overcoming.co.uk

First published in the UK by Robinson,
an imprint of Constable & Robinson Ltd 2007

Important Note
This book is not intended as a substitute for medical advice or treatment.
Any person with a condition requiring medical attention should consult
a qualified medical practitioner or suitable therapist.

ISBN: 978-1-84529-236-2 (PACK ISBN)

ISBN: 978-1-84529-506-6 (PART ONE)

ISBN: 978-1-84529-507-3 (PART TWO)

ISBN: 978-1-84529-508-0 (PART THREE)

Printed and bound in the EU

1 3 5 7 9 10 8 6 4 2

Contents

Note to Practitioners

This self-help course is suitable for a wide range of reading abilities and its step-by-step format makes it ideal for working through alone or under supervision. The course is divided into three workbooks, and each contains a full supply of worksheets and charts to be filled in on the page – so there is no need for photocopying. If you do decide to photocopy this material you will need to seek the permission of the publishers to avoid a breach of copyright law.

Introduction: How to Use this Workbook

What's in the workbooks?

This self-help course aims to give people with bulimia nervosa and binge-eating problems a way towards recovery. It is divided into three parts.

Part One explains:

- what bulimia nervosa and binge-eating problems are;
- how they affect people;
- what causes them;
- whether and how you might benefit from the self-help course.

Part Two explains:

- how to set about using the self-help course;
- how to monitor what you eat;
- how to plan your eating;
- how to learn to prevent binges.

Part Three explains:

- how to learn problem-solving skills;
- how to stop dieting;
- how to change how you think;

and also contains a section of useful information.

How long will the course take?

It is not possible to say exactly how long it will take you to work through this self-help course. Different people find different parts easier to manage, and most people hit sticky patches where they need to spend longer working on one task or stage. Don't feel under pressure to move on before you are ready. As a rule of thumb, the whole course usually takes three to six months to complete. But you may need longer than this. Take your time, and go at what feels the right pace for you.

How do I use the books?

These workbooks are just that – books for working in. So feel free to write on them! Don't just fill in the question boxes, worksheets and charts, but make notes in the margins, underline things you think are important, or mark things you don't quite understand and want to come back to. We have provided a few extra pages for your thoughts and reflections at the back of each workbook, should you need extra space.

Will it work for me?

The self-help principles presented in Parts Two and Three of this course are based on cognitive behavioural therapy, a well-tested and proven form of psychological therapy that helps you deal with problems in a very practical and personal way. These principles have been used by many people with bulimia nervosa and binge-eating problems to help them towards recovery. It has been shown in recent research that the great majority of people with bulimia nervosa and binge-eating problems also benefit from these principles when they are accessed via the self-help programme outlined below.

How will I know if I've recovered?

It is important to be clear about what 'recovery' from bulimia nervosa means. Many people do recover fully. They find they can eat normally without anxiety and without the concerns about their weight and shape which used to dominate their lives.

However, many people find they still sometimes have difficulties with food and related concerns, even if these problems only surface on rare occasions of stress. If you find that these difficulties still come up from time to time, this does not mean that you have not recovered. Part of a realistic notion of recovery is accepting that difficulties with eating may occasionally come back, but that they can be dealt with using the principles set out in this course.

Using the book to help someone else

- This book is intended mainly for people who have bulimia nervosa or binge-eating problems themselves. However, it will also be helpful to others. The families and friends of people who binge often want to know more about the problem.

- If you are using the course yourself, it may well be helpful if someone else – a parent, partner or friend – knows what you are trying to do so that they can help and support you.

- Finally, it is suggested in the self-help course that the person using it gets someone to help them. This could be a friend or relative, but it is even better if it is someone less close to them, such as a general practitioner, a nurse or a dietitian. This person will need to know what advice is contained in the course if they are to give the most help they can.

A note on gender

Because most people who binge and/or suffer from bulimia nervosa are women, the user of these books is referred to in the text as 'she' and 'her'. This is by no means intended to imply that the course is directed only at women; some men also suffer from these problems, and they are just as likely to benefit from following this programme.

SECTION 1: Problem Solving

Note: Read through all of this section before you start to put it into action.

It is very common for people with difficulties controlling their eating to binge in response to all sorts of problems that overwhelm them. These problems may be directly to do with food and eating, but they may also concern other aspects of life: work, family, friends and so on. So it is important that as part of your work towards recovery you develop a strategy for identifying problems, addressing them, and generating solutions other than eating.

Sometimes it's easy to see a problem coming up: for example, you might notice, when making plans for the next day, that some event represents a potential obstacle to your meal plan. Perhaps a friend you have not seen for a long time has announced that she will drop round and you feel that there is an expectation that you should make a special meal or cake for the occasion; or you know you will be extremely nervous because of a job interview in the afternoon and will not feel like eating all day.

Make a note here of a couple of the kinds of problem that you have found in the past tended to trigger a binge. Try to recall one directly related to eating and one related to some other area of life:

Eating-related problem leading to binge:

_____

_____

Non-eating-related problem leading to binge:

_____

_____

At other times it's not to easy to be that precise about the source of the problem. You may feel anxious or miserable and know that this makes you vulnerable to the impulse to overeat. It is easy to identify the problem as an urge to overeat, when the real problem is whatever it is that is making you feel anxious or depressed.

For many people with eating problems the urge to overeat is an automatic response to problems of any kind. When such an urge arises, it is important to ask yourself the question: *'Why do I have an urge to overeat **now**? What is the problem that lies behind this feeling?'* Of course, in the past the answer to this question often will have been that you have not eaten enough (or at all). But if you are sticking to your meal plan and eating a reasonable amount of food, then there must be some other answer. It is important for you to try to find out what the basic problem is. Once you have done so, you will be in a position to deal with the problem and you will not then automatically overeat. The following section shows a tried and tested method of doing this.

The five steps in problem solving

Once you have identified what the problem is:

1 Write the *problem* out as clearly as you can. You will already have noted it briefly in the final column of your monitoring sheet; now take a new sheet of paper so that you have all the space you need. If there is more than one problem, try to untangle the problems into separate ones; then deal with these individually.

2 Now write down as many *alternative solutions* to the problem as you can think of. Don't hold back or censor yourself; you want to be able to look at all possible solutions. Don't worry for the moment whether they seem sensible or not.

3 Look at each of your possible solutions and think about its *implications*; that is, precisely what would be involved, whether you realistically could see it through, and whether it is likely to be effective in dealing with the problem.

4 Choose what looks to you like the best solution (or combination of solutions) and *decide* to act on it.

5 At the end of the day, *evaluate* what has happened. Was your chosen solution effective? If it did not work out as it was supposed to, try to think what you might have done to produce a better outcome.

This blow-by-blow description may make problem solving look rather tedious and somewhat complicated. In fact, it is a very effective technique and, with a little practice, it can be managed quite easily. The box opposite shows two examples of how one person with bulimia nervosa identified problems and worked through the problem solving process, together with a statement of the outcome or 'evaluation'.

a **Food-related problem: evening meal with friend cancelled at last moment.**

b **Non-food-related problem: left house keys at work.**

1 Problem: *What am I going to do about eating?*

1 Problem: *Feeling panicky (and like eating) because I don't know how I am going to get in.*

2 Alternative solutions:
a) *eat at home – left over food*
b) *eat at home – get take-out*
c) *avoid eating altogether*
d) *arrange to eat with friends*

2 Alternative solutions:
a) *return to work to get keys*
b) *break in window at back of house*
c) *wait outside until others return*
d) *visit friend and return later*
e) *leave note on door*

3 Implications:
a) *OK, could treat myself to a drink*
b) *raining, and take-out too large*
c) *too much restraint, probably end up overeating*
d) *would be a good way to spend the evening*

3 Implications:
a) *probably no one left at work so will not be able to get in*
b) *a bit drastic, too expensive to repair*
c) *it may be a very long wait in the cold*
d) *would be good to visit Sue, hope she's in*
e) *good idea, leave possible phone numbers of where I'll be*

4 Decision: *Do (d) and if that's not possible will do (a)*

4 Decision: *Will do (d) and (e)*

5 Evaluation: *Friends couldn't make it – had leftovers and drink, successful*

5 Evaluation: *Sue not in, visited Steve instead, Clare saw my note and phoned within an hour to say she was home. Felt good, hadn't panicked and hadn't eaten.*

For some people, problem solving in this way comes very easily. They find that it is essentially a more structured way of what they had been doing in their heads already. For them, the benefits of problem solving more formally will be obvious and they will experience these benefits rapidly.

For others, formal problem solving feels very strange, even alien to their usual way of thinking and behaving. For them, it is likely to be more of a struggle to use this technique effectively. However, it is worth persevering because this technique is a very powerful one that has helped many people.

On pages 6 and 7 two boxes are provided headed 'Problem solving' and with the headings for the five steps provided. Use these to try out the problem-solving technique in the way described. (More blank 'Problem solving' forms are provided at the back of this workbook.) Over the course of the next week, on two occasions identify a problem and try to come to a resolution, using the spaces provided to work through the process as described above. Then take these to your 'helper' and talk them over together. This can be especially useful if you have gone through a problem-solving exercise and found that your chosen solution has not worked. You will then be able to look at what other options you might have considered and how this might have affected the outcome.

Problems with depression

Feeling depressed can be a major obstacle to overcoming eating difficulties. People sometimes react to relatively minor setbacks in their efforts to deal with their eating problems by becoming totally demoralized and fiercely self-critical. As a result, their confidence and strength of purpose are undermined and they find it even harder to control their eating.

It is important to accept that overcoming your problems with eating is likely to be a struggle and that you will inevitably not succeed all the time in everything you are trying to do. If you succeed at *something* you are making some progress, and you should give yourself credit for this; and where you do not succeed, if you reflect on why this happened rather than simply condemning yourself, you can learn something which can help you in the future.

Sometimes more general feelings of depression, not specifically related to eating or weight concerns, also lower morale and make it hard to control eating. If you can see from your monitoring sheets that this is a pattern in your experience, try to think what it is that is making you feel depressed. Treat it as a 'problem' in the manner described above and try to find solutions. You might find a self-help book useful, such as Paul Gilbert's *Overcoming Depression* (for full publication details see Section 4 of this workbook entitled 'Useful Information').

Occasionally, people are so depressed that they are seriously incapacitated. Their symptoms may include:

- not sleeping properly;

- waking up early in the morning;

- feeling tired all the time and completely without energy;

- finding it impossible to concentrate because of preoccupation with gloomy thoughts and consequently impossible to work;

- being unable to see any hope in the future for themselves and feeling that life is not worth living.

If you are persistently experiencing some or all of these symptoms it is important that you get help. Go and talk to your doctor soon. Once you have begun to get professional help with your depression, your mood will improve and you will then be able to make use of this manual and deal with your eating problems.

Problems with relationships

It is common for people who are monitoring their eating to find that binges are triggered by problems in their relationships with their parents, husbands or boyfriends, or other close friends. If you find that this is the case for you, it is worth using the problem-solving technique described above to pinpoint exactly what the nature of the difficulty is and what you can do about it.

Again, your monitoring sheets will often show patterns which make it clear where the problem lies. It could be something very specific, like your mother unwittingly forcing you to eat food you do not want; or it might concern a more general issue with parents, such as difficulties with independence. Similarly, with a husband or boyfriend it could relate to something concerning eating, or some more general aspect of your relationship. There are, of course, any number of possibilities here. The point is that by writing down what the nature of the problem is and by thinking about what sorts of solutions might be possible, you offer yourself the chance to break a cycle in both your eating problems and your relationships. You may even decide that your relationship problems are of such importance that you should seek professional help in resolving them.

Problem solving

Problem:

Alternative solutions:

Implications:

Decision:

Evaluation:

Problem solving

Problem:

Alternative solutions:

Implications:

Decision:

Evaluation:

The examples on pages 10 and 11 show how one person pinpointed a problem on her monitoring sheet and applied the problem-solving technique to deal with it.

Problems with feeling fat

It is very common for people who have difficulties controlling their eating to say that they often feel fat, and that this feeling makes them diet; but at the same time, feeling fat distresses them and makes them want to eat. Most people do not question this feeling, simply assuming that it is a genuine reflection of the state of their body.

However, if you record on your monitoring sheet every time you have a strong sense of feeling fat, it is likely that when you look over your sheets you will discover that this feeling arises in all sorts of different contexts, some of which are clearly related to circumstances surrounding food (such as having just eaten a meal) or shape (such as wearing a tight dress or going out with a thin friend), but many of which have nothing at all to do with food or eating. In fact, you may well discover that, like so many people whose eating is out of control, for you 'feeling fat' has come to be an automatic response to any negative emotion. *You may just feel 'bad' and immediately convert this into feeling 'fat'.*

There are many events or circumstances which could be responsible for your feeling bad, and they should be recognized for what they are, addressed and resolved. The way to proceed is to record on your monitoring sheet whenever you feel fat and ask yourself: *'What is the real problem that is making me feel bad?'* Once you have pinpointed the problem, you will be in a position to think about appropriate solutions.

You might find it helpful to look over a week's worth of your monitoring sheets and jot down a couple of the different situations in which you have noted that you 'feel fat'. Then, try to work out what the real problem is and write it in the space below. Then, taking each in turn, apply the problem-solving technique and see if you can work out a solution.

When did I 'feel fat'? What was happening?   *What is the real problem here?*

(1) _____   _____

_____   _____

(2) _____   _____

_____   _____

Problems with feeding other people

Preparing food for friends or relatives and eating with them should be a pleasurable experience. But it can be a nightmare for people with bulimia nervosa. All sorts of basic issues cause anxiety and confusion, such as:

- *'What shall I cook?'*

- *'How much should I prepare?'*

- *'Do I serve everyone's food myself or do I leave them to do it for themselves?'*

- *'What size helpings should I serve?'*

- *'Do I offer second helpings and, if so, how forcefully?'*

- *'How long should the meal take?'*

- *'What do I do with leftover food?'*

These questions all pose serious problems; but each of them can be solved using the technique described above.

Two general principles might be helpful.

- First, try to avoid doing anything which you know will create difficulties for you. So, if you are preparing a special three-course meal and including a conventional dessert would be a problem, why not prepare some exotic fruit instead? And, if leftovers are going to be difficult for you to resist, arrange for someone else to remove them or, if this is not possible, throw them away.

- Second, as a general rule it is a good idea to treat others as you would like to be treated yourself. So, for example, do not force food on to people and give them as much choice as possible about what and how much they eat.

Monitoring sheet

Meal Plan

Date: 14th October   **Day:** Thursday

7.30am Breakfast: Bran cereal with banana and milk   4.30pm Snack: Crunchy bar

10.00am Snack: Apple   7.00pm Supper: Steamed fish, new potatoes, beans, tomato salad

1.00pm Lunch: Boiled egg on toast and yogurt   10.30pm Snack: Mango

Time	Food and liquid consumed	Place	B	C	Context of /feelings
7.30	Bran cereal with 2 bananas and milk	Kitchen			Mum insisted I have 2 bananas; so cross, I've now eaten far too much already.
1.00	Boiled egg on toast	Office			Shouldn't be eating this really, as I had too much at breakfast; feel so frustrated. No yoghurt, anyway. Feel like I'm going to gain weight.
1.30	Cheese sandwich Packet crisps 2 Kit-Kats	Park	* * *		Went and bought food from corner shop and ate in lunch break; fed up and don't care.
7.00	Steamed fish New potatoes, beans Tomato salad Coffee	Dining room			Managed to eat planned meal, but now feel too full and fat and in a bad mood with Mum for ruining the day's eating.

Problem solving

Problem:

Mum doesn't think I eat enough at breakfast and keeps trying to make me eat more; if I do it ruins my meal plan and makes it really hard for me to stick to it for the rest of the day.

Alternative solutions:

(a) Make up for eating more at breakfast by missing morning snack or eating less lunch.

(b) Refuse to eat what Mum tries to make me eat in the morning.

(c) Just eat the bigger breakfast and carry on with the rest of the day as planned as well.

(d) Take Mum through the 'Note for helpers' again and try to explain better to her what I'm doing.

Implications:

(a) Would make me feel better in the short term, but then I'd be hungry and tempted to binge later. Would mean I'm not following the meal plan properly.

(b) That will just lead to rows and Mum will be worried and I'll feel guilty and tense and even more likely to overeat.

(c) I could do this but I'd still worry about gaining weight and that would make me tense and anxious and likely to overeat.

(d) Not easy as she finds it hard to understand why I can't just eat normal meals, but she does worry about me and wants to help and we'd both be relieved to talk about it properly.

Decision:

(d) seems the only one that is going to sort this out long-term, but it's not easy. Will try (d), and also (c) sometimes – that is, I'll tell her I'll eat bigger breakfasts at weekends if she won't press me in the week. Will have to choose a good moment.

Evaluation:

Friday morning ate the second banana and tried very hard not to panic in reaction, having decided to talk to Mum on Saturday. Had a good chat and went over the 'Note for helpers' together. Think we both understand each other's anxieties better now. Feel relieved.

Before you move on

Before moving on to the next step of the course in Section 2, ask yourself the following questions:

Have I been identifying problems which make me feel upset
(e.g. sad, anxious, angry), or make we want to binge,
and been writing them down?   YES / NO

Have I been using the problem-solving technique as a way of trying
to deal effectively with these problems?   YES / NO

Have I found that, by writing down the problem and attempting
to solve it, on some occasions I am able to deal with difficulties
which in the past would have led to binges?   YES / NO

If you can answer '*yes*' to all these questions, you should move on to Section 2. If you cannot answer '*yes*' to all the questions, you should re-read this section and try again to follow all the guidelines it contains.

SECTION 2: How to Stop Dieting

Note: Read through all of this section before you start to put it into action.

Perhaps you have managed to stick to your meal plan by eating a fairly restricted diet. So, you may well be managing to stick to three meals and two or three snacks a day, and by doing this you may well have stopped binge-eating or reduced it to a rare event. But there are two problems with this:

- While you are still only eating small quantities of low-calorie food, your control will remain precarious.

- The effort involved in sticking to such a regime will mean that you will go on being preoccupied with thoughts about food and eating – in fact, you may become even more preoccupied with these thoughts.

To continue your progress, therefore, *it is essential that you make a real effort to stop dieting*.

The three ways of dieting

There are essentially three ways in which people diet:

1 *Fasting*: that is, simply trying not to eat; going for long periods, even days, without eating. If you are following your meal plan, you won't be doing this by now.

2 *Eating too little*: for example, attempting to eat less than 1,000 calories a day. This method of dieting will have to go if you are to be sure of avoiding binges.

3 *Avoiding particular types of food*: this often involves forbidding yourself particular foods which are high in calories or which you feel make you binge. This method will also have to go because, as long as you retain the concept of 'bad' foods, or 'forbidden' foods, or 'banned' foods, or 'dangerous' foods, or 'binge' foods, or whatever you call them, you will be vulnerable to binge-eating under certain circumstances.

Are you ready to stop dieting?

At this point it is worth emphasizing that you must follow the programme in stages and make definite progress at each stage before moving on. Specifically, you should not attempt to deal with your desire to diet until you have

- managed to set up and keep to a regular meal plan and, as a result,

- established a more normal pattern of eating, as described in Part Two of this course.

This could take anything from two weeks to a few months, depending on the point at which you started. It's impossible to set a definite rule for when you will be ready to move on to this section, but, as a general guideline, if you are sticking to your meal plan and not binge-eating on most days you are probably ready to start tackling the dieting.

Tackling the three kinds of dieting

Fasting

The meal plan has dealt with the first method of dieting: that is, now you are eating regular meals and snacks, you will not be fasting.

Eating too little

It is often very difficult for someone who has been trying to restrict the amount they eat for a long time to have any idea of what constitutes a 'normal' amount of food. In fact, people vary considerably in how much food they need, and no strict rules can be provided that would apply to everyone.

So how can you discover what is a 'normal', sensible amount to eat? There are several ways, best used in combination:

- Experiment and discover for yourself what is right for you. Try eating a little bit more at mealtimes, or more substantial snacks.

- Look at how much others eat.

- Talk to someone you trust about this and ask them to advise and help you.

A word of caution must be added here. Many women diet, and it would not help you to try to copy the eating habits of someone who is restricting her eating. In choosing a friend with whom to discuss this matter and perhaps share meals, try to find someone who is not overly concerned about her weight and who is not dieting.

It would be a mistake to try to deal with the problem of deciding how much to eat by trying to follow some exact formula. In the end you must come to know what amounts are right for you at each meal and snack. To start with, this kind of knowledge may seem simply beyond reach, and you may feel you must have some guidance, if only to give you a start. If you feel like this, you may find the box overleaf helpful. This sets out, as a very rough guide, an account of three days of 'normal' eating.

The amount of food set out here is roughly what a woman of average weight who is eating normally would eat. The relative proportions of fat, carbohydrate and protein are also typical of someone whose eating habits are perfectly normal.

Remember: *these three examples are just illustrations – you should definitely **not** copy them*. You may well need to eat more than is shown here, and you should not be alarmed if this is the case.

Avoiding particular types of food

When you look over your monitoring sheets you will see that the foods you eat in a binge are usually those very foods you are especially attempting to exclude from your diet because they are 'fattening' or because you think that they trigger binges. It is very common for people to say 'I never eat chocolate' and then to discover that their binges contain a variety of chocolate bars.

It is important that you come to be able to eat in moderation those foods you are avoiding.

Only by doing this can you ultimately make a rational choice about what you want to eat. If you continue to avoid particular 'dangerous' foods, there will always be the threat that if you are presented with them you will binge. It is worth making the point here that:

No food is in itself fattening; and, conversely, eating too much of any food can be fattening.

Day 1

Breakfast: one Weetabix/half-cup of Wheaties with milk, orange, cup of coffee

Mid-morning: apple, cup of tea

Lunch: ham, tomato and cucumber sandwich (two slices of bread), packet of crisps, fruit yogurt, carton of fruit juice

Mid-afternoon: two chocolate digestive biscuits, cup of tea

Evening meal: grilled chicken breast, three boiled potatoes, portion of peas, portion of carrots, glass of fruit juice, bowl of fruit salad, cup of tea

Bedtime: two biscuits, hot chocolate drink

Day 2

Breakfast: bowl of cornflakes with milk, a slice of toast with margarine and marmalade, glass of fruit juice

Mid-morning: chocolate digestive biscuits, cup of tea

Lunch: Marmite or vegetable paté sandwich (two slices of bread), apple, slice of fruit cake, carton of fruit juice

Mid-afternoon: Mars bar, cup of tea

Evening meal: baked potato with margarine and cheddar cheese, side salad, stewed apple, cup of tea

Bedtime: scone with margarine, cup of tea

Day 3

Breakfast: two slices of toast with margarine and marmalade, glass of fruit juice, cup of tea

Mid-morning: two digestive biscuits, cup of tea

Lunch: bowl of tomato soup, two slices of bread with margarine, cup of coffee

Mid-afternoon: scone with margarine, cup of tea

Evening meal: cod steak with cheese sauce, two scoops of mashed potato, portion of broccoli, one grilled tomato, bowl of canned or fresh fruit

Bedtime: slice of toast with margarine, hot chocolate drink

If you are still concerned that eating even a small amount of your 'forbidden' foods might make you gain weight, you might want to try a small experiment to convince yourself that this is really not the case. This experiment will involve weighing yourself more frequently than usual for a short period. Let's say that chocolate bars rank among your most 'difficult' foods. So:

- Decide to have a bar of chocolate on a particular day.

- Weigh yourself on that day before eating the chocolate and record your weight on your monitoring sheet.

- Then weigh yourself the next morning and record that weight.

You will find that, contrary to your fears, eating the chocolate bar the previous day has made no difference to your weight.

Acquiring this sort of concrete proof may seem silly, but can be very effective in challenging irrational but habitual and powerful fears about the fattening effects of particular foods.

You may still argue that, although one chocolate bar makes no difference to your weight and shape, you would certainly become fatter if you were to eat many of them every day. And you may be afraid that if you allowed yourself to eat any chocolate at all, you would be unable to control yourself and would eat large amounts constantly.

This fear comes from your previous experience of resisting eating forbidden foods only to find that you then ate large amounts of these foods in binges. It is very important to realize that *the reason you ate large quantities of 'forbidden' food in binges was precisely because you avoided them at other times*. Although this may seem difficult to accept, if you examine your monitoring sheets you will see that it is clearly the case. The truth is that if you widen your diet and get rid of the idea of 'forbidden foods', you will be less likely to binge.

The process of widening the range of foods you eat is a difficult one and, if things go wrong, it can create new problems. For this reason a set of precise guidelines is set out below, and it is strongly advised that you follow these closely and carefully. To some people this may seem over-cautious, but there are potential pitfalls in this process – and why run unnecessary risks when you have already come so far?

1 Draw up a list of those foods you are avoiding either because you feel they are too 'fattening' or because you believe they invariably, or often, trigger binges. If you find this task difficult, take a trip to a supermarket, armed with only a pen and paper (definitely no money), and wander around the food section examining the shelf contents and writing down all the items you would avoid for these reasons.

2 Organize the list into a specific order or hierarchy, with the item that presents the least difficulty (i.e. the one you regard as least 'fattening' or threatening) at the bottom and the one that presents the most difficulty at the top.

3 Divide the hierarchy into three classes of difficulty, grouping together those items that would cause you slight difficulty, those that would cause moderate difficulty, and those that would cause extreme difficulty. The box on page 19 contains an example of what such a hierarchy might look like; but, obviously, every person's list would be different.

Using the blank box on page 20, create your own hierarchy of difficult foods in the way described above.

4 Now start to incorporate some of these foods into your meal plans. Beginning with the group of foods which you have listed as 'slightly difficult', plan to eat one item from the list as part of a planned meal or snack every second or third day. Start with the least difficult item in the group.

It is important that you plan to do this at a time when you feel that you will be particularly safe, such as when you are eating with a friend or when it would be impossible for you to get at other food supplies. If, when the time comes, you have any doubts about whether you will be able to manage to eat the particular item without losing control afterwards, then do not eat it. If necessary, throw it away.

Stick with the 'slightly difficult' group until you can to eat any item in it without difficulty and you feel that they ought no longer to be on your list of avoided foods. Once you are comfortable with the food in the first class, those items which used to present slight difficulty, you can go on to the 'moderately difficult' class; and then, eventually, to the 'extremely difficult' group.

It is not possible to say how long this will take. But two or three weeks at each level is probably how long most people will need. Some will be able to move up the hierarchy more quickly than this and some will need to move more slowly. However, it is much better to proceed with too much caution and to remain with the 'slightly difficult' class for an extra week, rather than move on when you are not really ready to do so. However long it takes, you should not move to a more difficult class of food until there is nothing you cannot eat without anxiety in the one you are tackling at present.

Hierarchy of 'difficult' foods

Extremely difficult:

1 Chocolate biscuits
2 Chips
3 Fancy cakes/desserts e.g. cheesecake
4 Chocolate bars
5 Sweets
6 Butter
7 Cream
8 Oil

Moderately difficult:

9   Pastry, e.g. pork pie or pizza, quiche, etc.
10 Jam, honey, marmalade
11 Crisps and nuts
12 Full fat cheese, e.g. Brie
13 Plain biscuits or cake
14 Cereal
15 Bread
16 Chinese egg roll
17 Bacon, ham, red meat, burgers, etc.
18 Savoury crackers
19 Ready-made sandwiches
20 Avocado

Slightly difficult:

21 Spaghetti, rice, pasta
22 Milk (full-fat)
23 Potatoes
24 Baked beans
25 Frozen yogurt
26 Bananas

Hierarchy of 'difficult' foods

Extremely difficult:

1

2

3

4

Moderately difficult:

1

2

3

4

Slightly difficult:

1

2

3

4

5 Finally, having learned that you can eat anything you want, you should decide roughly how often you would like to eat that sort of food and in what quantity. Clearly, it would be unwise to fill your day with the high-calorie and bulk food you previously ate in binges. It would also not be healthy. But it is important to remember that if you decide never to eat these foods at all, they will go back to being a threat to your control over your eating.

For example, if you used to avoid chocolate, it might be sensible to decide to have a chocolate bar as 'dessert' for lunch or as a mid-afternoon snack three or four times a week. Again, if this prospect is alarming to you, it is worth reminding yourself that eating three or four chocolate bars (or whatever food makes you particularly anxious) a week as part of controlled, binge-free eating is probably a tiny fraction of the number you would be eating if you were still bingeing.

The time taken to eliminate dieting is really not important, provided progress is being made; and progress means being able to eat a wider and wider range of food without fear, until you can eat anything, in moderation, without becoming afraid that it will cause you to get fat or to lose control and binge.

If you are not sure whether you have reached this point, it might be helpful to ask yourself:

- *'Could I go out for dinner to a restaurant with a group of people, with whom I am comfortable but whom I do not know well, and order a three-course meal?'* or

- *'Could I go to a dinner party with friends and eat whatever was served?'*

If you are able to say to yourself: *'Neither of these situations would present a serious problem to me because I can eat anything I like without overeating and without it making me fat,'* then this particular job is done.

Being able to cope in all situations

You may be unsure how to judge the significance of the progress you have made. You may have reached the point where:

- You can stick to your meal plan.

- You no longer binge or have the urge to overeat.

- There are no foods that you cannot include in moderation in your meal plan.

While this would be wonderful progress, there are two further issues which need to be addressed. One concerns your ideas and beliefs about weight and shape, and we'll come on to this in Section 3 below. The other concerns your ability to deal with all situations in which food has previously presented you with difficulty. Such situations may well include:

- those where you have to eat food someone else has prepared and served, so you have no control over what's gone into it, how much is in front of you or how many calories there are in it;

- those where you have to eat in public, for example dinner parties or work events;

- those where small amounts of food keep appearing, such as drinks parties, or where virtually limitless amounts of food are laid out, such as buffets.

If you are to be completely secure about your eating you will need to feel able to deal with all these situations, and any others that might now cause you anxiety about eating.

The way to do this is by following the same principles as outlined above for gradually including all sorts of food in what you eat. This time:

- Make a list of all the situations you know you would find difficult.

- Then practise coping in them under safe circumstances, starting with the least threatening and gradually move on until you feel able to manage any situation in which you might find yourself.

An example of one person's list of difficult situations is shown opposite. After that there is a blank box headed 'Difficult situations' for you to use to compile your own list. Write down in this box as many different situations as you can think of where you might have problems in dealing with food. Then, starting with the least threatening situation at the bottom of the list and working upwards, whenever you are able to do so, try coping in the particular circumstance and make some notes about how you have managed. (You might not be able to work through them all strictly in order – after all, none of us is invited to a wedding every month! But try not to make too big a jump up from a less difficult to a very difficult situation.) Another blank form headed 'Coping with a difficult situation' is provided on page 24 for you to do this, and there are more copies of this at the end of this workbook.

Difficult situations

In order from most difficult (1) down to least difficult (8).

1 *Going out to a dinner party*
2 *Going to Sunday lunch with parents-in-law*
3 *Having a meal at a restaurant with friends*
4 *Going to a buffet wedding reception*
5 *Going to a drinks party with snacks handed round*
6 *Drinking in a bar with friends where there are snacks available*
7 *Having a meal at a restaurant with friends*
8 *Eating in the cafeteria at work*

Difficult situations

In order from most difficult (1) down to least difficult (8) – you may have more or fewer than 8.

1 _____

2 _____

3 _____

4 _____

5 _____

6 _____

7 _____

8

Coping with a difficult situation

Difficult situation:

_____

_____

Level of difficulty (tick one):

☐ mild

☐ moderate

☐ severe

Notes on how I managed:

_____

_____

_____

_____

_____

_____

_____

_____

_____

_____

_____

_____

_____

Before you move on

Before moving on to the next step of the course in Section 3, ask yourself the following questions:

Have I considered whether I have been eating enough food in my meals
and snacks and, if necessary, made changes to how much I eat?   YES / NO

Have I considered which foods I avoid because they are 'dangerous',
and instituted a programme for introducing these foods into my
normal eating?   YES / NO

Have I practised eating in a range of situations which previously
would have presented me with difficulty?   YES / NO

If you can answer '*yes*' to these questions, you should go on to Section 3. However, Section 2 is only successfully completed when you can also answer '*yes*' to the question:

Am I able to eat in a controlled way, and in reasonable quantities,
any food that I like?   YES / NO

If you can answer '*yes*' to all the above questions, you have successfully completed Section 2. However, if you can answer '*yes*' to any of the questions, you have made some progress and, though you should go on working on this section, you can proceed to the next step as well.

SECTION 3: How to Change Your Mind

If you had not been concerned about your weight and shape in the first place, almost certainly you would never have started dieting and would never have lost control of your eating and experienced all the problems that followed. In some sense, to put your eating problems behind you completely, *you need to change your mind about how important weight and shape are to you.*

This is not to say that your weight and shape should become *unimportant* to you: nearly all women in our society are concerned about their weight and shape to some extent, and it would not be realistic to expect you to become less concerned than is usual. However, you do need to reduce the intensity and prominence of these concerns, so that they no longer dominate your life and dictate how you behave, especially how you eat.

Clearly, this is going to be a long and difficult task. Some people find that, as their eating becomes increasingly 'normal', and there is space in their lives for them to develop their interests and commitments, their concerns about weight and shape naturally become increasingly less important. Others have to give special attention to changing the way they think about themselves and the importance of their shape and weight. This section sets out some suggestions and guidelines as to how you might do this most effectively.

Reading about why weight and shape seem so important

There are a number of books which deal with the question of why weight and shape are of such major importance to women. Most of these are feminist works which expose the social pressures to be thin and the consequent tyranny under which women suffer. It is worth reading one or two of these books and considering the wider social origins of women's weight and shape concerns. Examples are Susie Orbach's *Fat is a Feminist Issue* and Naomi Wolf's *The Beauty Myth*. For full publication details of these and other relevant books, see Section 4 of this workbook entitled 'Useful Information'.

Questioning the importance of weight and shape

At present, how you feel about your weight and shape is probably central to how worthwhile you feel you are as a person. If your weight falls, you feel you are a better person; and if your weight rises, you feel a failure, incompetent and unlikeable. You can judge the extent to which this is true for you by examining your monitoring sheets to see how you have felt after weighing yourself. *This tendency to judge self-worth in terms of weight and shape almost always underlies eating problems*. Indeed, it is probably because you held these attitudes that you began dieting in the first place, and because of these attitudes that you continue to be so deeply concerned about your weight and shape. If you can reduce the intensity of these concerns, you will find it easier to maintain control of your eating. To do this, you will need to reconsider the link between your self-esteem and the shape or weight of your body.

What do you value in people?

One way of doing this is to make a list of the attributes which you consider valuable in other people. What things do you value about your friends, for example? Such a list might include things like:

- their reliability and trustworthiness;

- their devotion to their children;

- their dedication to their work;

- their sense of fun;

- their thoughtfulness to their friends;

and so on. It is likely that their physical appearance, and especially their weight and shape, would rank very low on your list of valued attributes. If you are not sure about this, ask yourself whether you would stop being a friend of, or start to despise, someone you know well if she were to gain, say, 10 pounds (while retaining all her other positive characteristics).

Try this with someone you know. Think of a particular individual you know and like, then list here the five things you value most in him or her:

_____

_____

_____

_____

_____

Now ask yourself:

Would I like _____ any less if s/he were to put on
10 pounds in weight?   YES/NO

Another useful thing you can do is to ask a trusted friend to provide you with a list of your 'good' and 'bad' qualities, as she sees them. Again, you would almost certainly find that your weight and shape do not feature prominently on either of these lists.

Valuing yourself as you value others

By doing these two simple exercises, you should come to realize that

- weight and shape are not important in how you value others; and

- weight and shape are not important in how others value you.

What you need to do next is to apply to yourself the same standards which you apply to others and which they apply to you.

Achieving this is not, of course, as simple as merely making a decision to think differently about yourself. The first step is to be aware of when you are exaggerating the importance of your weight and shape. You can do this by recording on your monitoring sheets times when you attribute negative events or feelings to your weight or shape, and then having a kind of debate with yourself to try and reach a more reasoned and rational perspective.

For example, if a person to whom you are attracted does not pay much attention to you at a social gathering, you might find that you instantly think something like: *'He's not interested in me because I'm too fat.'* If you reflect on this, you will probably be able to think of many other possible reasons why he behaved as he did, including reasons that have nothing at all to do with you.

Overleaf is an example of how you might note such an event and reflect on it, followed by a blank box for you to try it for yourself. More blank sheets are provided at the back of this workbook.

Exaggerating the importance of weight and shape

Occasion:

Interview for promotion at work. I'd made a real effort to present myself well, but the interviewer was very stony-faced and didn't seem to respond to anything I said.

Initial reaction:

She despised me because I'm too fat.

Other possible explanations:

They've already decided to give the job to someone else.

My qualifications aren't suitable for the job.

It's a bit soon for me to be applying for promotion anyway.

The interviewer had a headache.

They've decided to promote me anyway and were only going through the motions.

Conclusion:

I still don't know whether I'll get the promotion, but whether I do or not it's unlikely to have anything to do with my weight or shape.

Exaggerating the importance of weight and shape

Occasion:

Initial reaction:

Other possible explanations:

Conclusion:

If you continue to monitor your reactions and deliberately look for other perspectives in this way, you will find that gradually your weight and shape will come not to loom so large in how you evaluate yourself and your circumstances.

Thinking about the way you think

People who have problems with eating often also hold more general styles of thinking that cause problems. Being aware of these in yourself, and working to change them, can help a great deal in trying to make concerns about weight and shape less prominent in your life. Two types of habitual ways of thinking seem particularly common.

Perfectionism

This is a tendency

- to have unrealistically high expectations of yourself, and

- to judge yourself unreasonably harshly.

You might find that over the years you have, consciously or not, developed a set of rules for yourself about how to behave or how to be as a person, and that you are particularly hard on yourself in judging whether you succeed or fail in living up to these rules. You might also find it hard to forgive yourself when you do make a mistake or fall short of a desired goal.

As an example, you might think 'It is wrong to get angry,' and then feel extremely guilty and self-critical when you do lose your temper, even in very provoking situations.

This harsh approach to your own ordinary human frailty connects with the eating problem by making you feel worse about yourself. This, in turn, makes you feel bad about your weight and shape, which makes you want to diet, which is the sure route to your binge-eating again. This in turn makes you feel guilty and condemn yourself, and so the cycle continues. Changing these unrealistic expectations and harsh judgements of yourself is not easy, but it is well worth the effort.

Again, you might begin by considering how you would evaluate a friend in similar circumstances.

- Would you condemn a friend for making a mistake?

- Would you be very critical of a friend for losing her temper in provoking circumstances, as in the example mentioned above?

In any situation where you feel guilty or self-condemnatory, ask yourself whether you would accept or forgive similar behaviour in your best friend and, if you would, try to apply the same sympathetic approach to yourself.

In effect, treat yourself as you would your own best friend.

'All-or-nothing' thinking

This is a tendency to view things in absolute, 'all-or-nothing' terms. This principally affects thinking about weight and shape and about eating, but it can also affect other aspects of life. For example, some people tend to see themselves at some times as a complete success and at other times as a total failure. In relation to their weight, they see themselves as either thin and attractive or fat and loathsome. They might think of a day when they ate very little as a great success and one where they ate a little more than they were happy with as a total disaster.

Thinking in this 'all-or-nothing', 'black-and-white' way can be a serious obstacle to progress in any area, and it would certainly hinder your efforts to establish normal eating and a healthy attitude to weight and shape. If, every time you fall a little short of what you are aiming at, you believe you have failed catastrophically, you can easily come to feel that you might as well give up altogether and stop even trying. In reality, things are never this clearly black and white. Every attempt, every achievement, falls somewhere between the two extremes of success and failure; and coming to judge your efforts and achievement more reasonably will help you greatly in maintaining control over your eating and over your concerns about weight and shape.

It is not easy to change an all-or-nothing style of thinking. However, it is possible to do so. Whenever you find yourself responding in an extremely negative way to a situation (e.g. 'This is a complete disaster' or 'This is absolutely terrible' or 'I am completely useless'), note the reaction on your monitoring sheet and then, just as you did when noting occasions when you exaggerated the importance of weight and shape, consider what evidence there might be against it. You will find that there is often considerable evidence against the catastrophic or disastrous conclusion; and if you allow yourself to consider alternative conclusions, you will be in a position to move forward positively.

Overleaf is an example of how you might note such an event and reflect on it, followed by a blank box for you to try it for yourself. More blank sheets are provided at the back of this workbook.

Challenging 'all-or-nothing' thinking

Occasion:

Coffee-time at work.
Someone gave me a piece of birthday cake and I ate it.

Initial reaction:

It wasn't on my meal plan; now I've ruined the whole day and might as well give up. Feel very tempted to binge.

Evidence against that reaction:

It was only one piece of cake, and I was going to have a biscuit as my planned snack anyway. If I just continue with my meal plan, I'll have had another good day. One piece of cake isn't going to make any difference to my weight — and anyway, I'm working on coping with unforeseen disruptions to my plan.

Conclusion:

It wasn't a disaster at all. At the very most it was a small departure from my plan, and in fact it was a useful opportunity to practise coping with an eating event I hadn't predicted.

Challenging 'all-or-nothing' thinking

Occasion:

Initial reaction:

_____

Evidence against that reaction:

Conclusion:

Attending a discussion group

There are a great many groups run by people with eating problems, where people meet to discuss their difficulties. Few people whose eating is seriously disturbed find that they can overcome their problems with food by attending such a group without seeking any other help. However, some people find that a group of this kind can be helpful. Sometimes, you can only see your own views and their implications clearly when you hear someone else expressing them. You might wish to consider attending such a group with this purpose in mind.

However, there is a danger of which you must be aware: many people have very strong views about why people have eating disorders and about what sort of help sufferers ought to be receiving. If you are attempting to overcome your eating problems on your own with the help of this manual, it will not help you to have your efforts undermined. Therefore, before you commit yourself to attending such a group it would be prudent to try to find out exactly what sort of group it is and what its purpose is. Information about groups can be obtained from eating disorders associations (see the list of addresses and telephone numbers given in Section 4 of this workbook, 'Useful Information').

Lapses and slippages

For people who overcome their problems with eating and resume 'normal' eating habits, it's always possible that control over eating may be disrupted again.

- You might find, for example, that after a year of normal eating, something stressful happens – you might have had an argument with your mother or your partner, or a particularly difficult period at work – and suddenly, out of the blue, you lose control of your eating and binge.

- Or you might, for a variety of reasons, gradually slip back into dieting; your weight may fall, and then suddenly you binge.

Whatever the circumstances of the lapse and whatever triggers it, the sudden return to binge-eating can be very distressing, and invariably the person concerned immediately concludes that she is back to square one. However, this is not so.

The important thing to remember is that the significance of such a lapse (and a lapse is all that it is) has less to do with what actually happens than with how you react to it.

So, if you react as if struck down by a catastrophe and go into a deep depression, resigning yourself to a lifetime of binge-eating, you may well find it very difficult to restore order to your eating habits. If, on the other hand, you are able to see that there were special circumstances that led to the lapse and that it represents an unfortunate minor setback *which you now have the skills and the will to overcome*, you will be able to get back on the track of normal eating quite quickly.

If you are at all concerned that you might be sliding back into old habits and feel at all vulnerable to overeating, you should immediately go back to this course and start again at the beginning of Part Two, Section 2: reinstate monitoring, work out a precise meal plan, plan your eating ahead of time, and so on. You will find after a few days of such effort that your confidence will return and you will again be able to be more relaxed about your eating.

Once your eating is under control, it is enormously tempting to say to yourself: 'Thank goodness that is over. Now I need never worry about my eating again.' This is a very natural and understandable reaction. However, you should be wary of it. The concerns about your weight and shape that were the driving force in your eating disorder, even if they seem to have disappeared, remain an area of vulnerability. So, at times of stress, when others in the same circumstances might become depressed or anxious or drink too heavily, you are liable to become concerned about your weight and shape and to want to diet. It is important that you are alert to such feelings and take steps to avoid acting on them. Indeed, if such concerns do arise you should treat them as a problem that needs to be dealt with formally (as described in Section 1 of this workbook). Watch out in particular for two danger signals:

- feeling badly about yourself because of dissatisfaction with your weight and shape; and

- the desire to diet.

Before you move on

Before deciding that you no longer need this manual because you consider yourself to have recovered, ask yourself the following questions:

Am I able to eat normally without worrying about the impact on my weight and shape?   YES / NO

Am I able to eat normally without strictly planning ahead and without keeping records?   YES / NO

Am I able to accept my own worth as a human being without this depending on my view of my weight and shape?   YES / NO

If you can answer 'yes' to these questions, it is safe to free yourself from the constraints of this manual and to begin to be more relaxed about your eating. However, should you experience any difficulty with eating in the future you should immediately put yourself back in 'treatment' using this course, and return to strictly following all the principles you have so effectively employed.

SECTION 4: Useful Information

Useful addresses

If you want to obtain information about the clinical services for eating disorders in your area, or about self-help groups, the following organizations will be able to help you:

Great Britain

Anorexia and Bulimia Care (ABC)
PO Box 173
Letchworth
Hertfordshire, SG6 1XQ
Tel: 01462 423 351
Email: anorexiabulimiacare@ntlworld.com
Website: www.anorexiabulimiacare.co.uk

British Association for Behavioural and Cognitive Psychotherapies (BABCP)
The Globe Centre
PO Box 9
Accrington, BB5 0XB
Tel/Fax: 01254 875 277/01254 239 114
Email: babcp@babcp.com
Website: www.babcp.org.uk

(BABCP have a list of cognitive behavioural therapists accredited by the organization)

British Association for Counselling and Psychotherapy (BACP)
BACP House
35-37 Albert Street
Rugby
Warwickshire, CV21 2SG
Tel/Fax: 0870 443 5252/0870 443 5161
Website: www.bacp.co.uk

British Psychological Society
St Andrew's House
48 Princess Road East
Leicester, LE1 7DR
Tel/Fax: 0116 254 9568/0116 247 0787
Email: mail@bps.org.uk
Website: www.bps.org.uk

(They hold a directory of chartered clinical psychologists, the people most likely in the UK to be trained in cognitive behavioural therapy)

Eating Disorders Association
103 Prince of Wales Road
Norwich, NR1 1DW
Tel/Fax: 01603 621 414/01603 664 915
Email: helpmail@edauk.com
Website: www.edauk.com

MIND: The National Association for Mental Health
Granta House
15-19 Broadway
Stratford
London, E15 4BQ
Infoline/Fax: 0845 766 0163/020 8522 1725
Email: contact@mind.org.uk
Website: www.mind.org.uk

National Centre for Eating Disorders
54 New Road
Esher
Surrey, KT10 9NU
Tel: 0845 838 2040
Website: www.eating-disorders.org.uk

NHS Direct
Tel: 0845 4647
Website: www.nhsdirect.nhs.uk

Oxford Cognitive Therapy Centre (OCTC)
Psychology Department
Warneford Hospital
Oxford, OX3 7JX
Tel/Fax: 01865 223 986/01865 226 411
Email: octc@obmh.nhs.uk
Website: www.octc.co.uk

Australia

Eating Disorders Foundation of Victoria, Inc.
1513 High Street
Glen Iris
Victoria 3146
Tel/Fax: 0061 3 9885 0318/0061 3 9885 1153
Email: edfv@eatingdisorders.org.au
Website: www.eatingdisorders.org.au

Canada

Anorexia Nervosa and Bulimia Association (ANAB)
767 Bayridge Drive
PO Box 30058
Kingston
Ontario, K7P 1CO
Tel: 001 613 547 3684
Email: anab@www.ams.queensu.ca
Website: www.phe.queensu.ca/anab/

USA

National Association of Anorexia Nervosa and Associated Disorders (ANAD)
PO Box 7
Highland Park, IL. 60035
Tel/Fax: 001 847 831 3438/001 847 433 4632
Email: anad20@aol.com
Website: www.anad.org

National Eating Disorders Association (NEDA)
603 Stewart Street
Suite 803
Seattle, WA98101
Toll-free information helpline: 001 800 931 2237
Email: info@NationalEatingDisorders.org
Website: www.nationaleatingdisorders.org

Useful books

Melanie Fennell, *Overcoming Low Self-Esteem*, London, Robinson, 1999

Paul Gilbert, *Overcoming Depression*, London, Robinson, 1997

Helen Kennerley, *Overcoming Anxiety*, London, Robinson, 1997

Susie Orbach, *Fat is a Feminist Issue*, London, Paddington, 1978

Naomi Wolf, *The Beauty Myth*, London, Vintage, 1991

A note for helpers

If you have been asked by someone with bulimia nervosa or a related problem to help them use this manual to overcome their problems with eating, please read the following paragraphs. These sketch out some general principles about how you might best be able to fulfil this role.

Is the course suitable for the person using it?

The course laid out in these workbooks is based on a self-help book that has been used to considerable benefit by a great many people with bulimia nervosa. It is therefore perfectly reasonable to expect that someone with bulimia nervosa or binge-eating problems who follows the course will benefit from it. However, it is obviously not the right way to proceed for everyone. In Part One, Section 4 of the course, a list is provided of kinds of people for whom the course is not appropriate. Before you begin helping someone to work through the course, you should consult this list and consider whether self-help is indeed appropriate for them. If you feel that it is not, clearly you must discuss this with the person you are trying to help and together you must come to a decision about the most appropriate course of action.

Do you need to know the whole course inside out?

If you are going to help someone use this manual, you should obviously be familiar with its contents. This does not mean that you must be an expert in the treatment of eating disorders. However, the self-help course does follow certain definite principles in a highly structured fashion, and you will need to be familiar with these basic principles. You won't, however, necessarily have to read the whole course at once; it is divided into clearly distinct steps in relatively small sections, and it would be possible, just before meeting someone you are helping, to skim through reasonably quickly the section with which they are concerned at the moment.

What can you do to help?

The most useful function that you can perform is to provide basic support and encouragement. There are bound to be times when someone trying to deal with her eating problems feels discouraged and even hopeless about ever significantly changing. It is at these times that the balanced perspective of an outsider can really help. When all one can see is one's failures, it can be immensely reassuring and helpful to be reminded of the successes one has had and the progress one has made.

It is important to emphasize that this course is a guide to *self*-help; and if you are assisting someone in using it, then you are helping her to help herself. So it is not your role to devise plans and strategies for her, but rather to encourage her to develop her own techniques for overcoming her difficulties. This does not mean, of course, that you should refuse to make any suggestions at all. There are times when, by looking through someone's monitoring sheets, you might, as an outsider, see certain patterns she has missed. If you spot anything you feel might be important, then obviously you should raise it. Similarly, certain points of detail, concerning, for example, the sort of food eaten or the timing of meals, may well seem to you worth mentioning and it is perfectly reasonable to do so. However, while you should feel free to make suggestions about prudent courses of action, in the end it is those strategies the person generates for herself which she is most likely to follow and which are therefore likely to be of most benefit to her. And, of course, in the end the decision whether to use whatever points you make is hers and not yours.

Overcoming bulimia nervosa is a struggle which will take many months. In the early stages of this self-help course it would be useful for the person using the manual to be able to see her helper often: weekly is probably best. Once some control over eating has been achieved, meetings can be held less frequently. However, it is important that the door is left open for help. This is especially important at times when someone who has been doing well experiences a lapse. If left entirely on her own she can become so disheartened that she gives up altogether, and what was really a minor lapse becomes a relapse. This doesn't need to happen; a couple of booster meetings with a helper is usually all that is needed to get the person back on the course to recovery.

Deciding to recruit a helper and make a genuine effort to use this manual to overcome eating problems is a brave decision. Anyone making that decision deserves a great deal of respect, support and encouragement. And with such help, she stands a good chance of making substantial improvement.

Extra Charts and Worksheets

46

Problem solving

Problem:

_____

Alternative solutions:

_____

Implications:

_____

Decision:

_____

Evaluation:

Problem solving

Problem:

Alternative solutions:

Implications:

Decision:

Evaluation:

48

Problem solving

Problem:

Alternative solutions:

Implications:

Decision:

Evaluation:

Problem solving

Problem:

Alternative solutions:

Implications:

Decision:

Evaluation:

Coping with a difficult situation

Difficult situation:

_____

_____

Level of difficulty (tick one):

☐ mild

☐ moderate

☐ severe

Notes on how I managed:

_____

_____

_____

_____

_____

_____

_____

_____

_____

_____

_____

_____

Coping with a difficult situation

Difficult situation:

_____

_____

Level of difficulty (tick one):

☐ mild

☐ moderate

☐ severe

Notes on how I managed:

_____

_____

_____

_____

_____

_____

_____

_____

_____

_____

_____

Coping with a difficult situation

Difficult situation:

_____

_____

Level of difficulty (tick one):

☐ mild

☐ moderate

☐ severe

Notes on how I managed:

_____

_____

_____

_____

_____

_____

_____

_____

_____

_____

_____

_____

_____

_____

Coping with a difficult situation

Difficult situation:

_____

_____

Level of difficulty (tick one):

☐ mild

☐ moderate

☐ severe

Notes on how I managed:

_____

_____

_____

_____

_____

_____

_____

_____

_____

_____

_____

54

Exaggerating the importance of weight and shape

Occasion:

Initial reaction:

Other possible explanations:

Conclusion:

Exaggerating the importance of weight and shape

Occasion:

Initial reaction:

Other possible explanations:

Conclusion:

Exaggerating the importance of weight and shape

Occasion:

Initial reaction:

Other possible explanations:

Conclusion:

Challenging 'all-or-nothing' thinking

Occasion:

Initial reaction:

Evidence against that reaction:

Conclusion:

58

Challenging 'all-or-nothing' thinking

Occasion:

Initial reaction:

Evidence against that reaction:

Conclusion:

Challenging 'all-or-nothing' thinking

Occasion:

Initial reaction:

Evidence against that reaction:

Conclusion:

Thoughts and Reflections

Order further books in the Overcoming series

Quantity	Title	Price	Total
	An Introduction to Coping with Anxiety (pack of 10 booklets)	£10.00	
	An Introduction to Coping with Depression (pack of 10 booklets)	£10.00	
	An Introduction to Coping with Health Anxiety (pack of 10 booklets)	£10.00	
	An Introduction to Coping with Panic (pack of 10 booklets)	£10.00	
	An Introduction to Coping with Phobias (pack of 10 booklets)	£10.00	
	An Introduction to Coping with Obsessive Compulsive Disorder (pack of 10 booklets)	£10.00	
	Overcoming Anxiety Self-Help Course	£21.00	
	Overcoming Low Self-Esteem Self-Help Course	£21.00	
	Overcoming Panic and Agoraphobia Self-Help Course	£21.00	
	Overcoming Social Anxiety and Shyness Self-Help Course	£21.00	
	Overcoming Anger and Irritability	£9.99	
	Overcoming Anorexia Nervosa	£9.99	
	Overcoming Anxiety	£9.99	
	Bulimia Nervosa and Binge-Eating	£9.99	
	Overcoming Childhood Trauma	£9.99	
	Overcoming Chronic Fatigue	£9.99	
	Overcoming Chronic Pain	£9.99	
	Overcoming Compulsive Gambling	£9.99	
	Overcoming Depression	£9.99	
	Overcoming Insomnia and Sleep Problems	£9.99	
	Overcoming Low Self-Esteem	£9.99	
	Overcoming Mood Swings	£9.99	
	Overcoming Obsessive Compulsive Disorders	£9.99	
	Overcoming Panic	£9.99	
	Overcoming Paranoid and Suspicious Thoughts	£9.99	
	Overcoming Problem Drinking	£9.99	
	Overcoming Relationship Problems	£9.99	
	Overcoming Sexual Problems	£9.99	
	Overcoming Social Anxiety and Shyness	£9.99	
	Overcoming Traumatic Stress	£9.99	
	Overcoming Weight Problems	£9.99	
	Overcoming Your Child's Fears and Worries	£9.99	
	Overcoming Your Smoking Habit	£9.99	
	P & P	FREE	
		Grand TOTAL £	

Name: _____

Delivery address: _____

_____

_____

Postcode: _____

Daytime tel. no.: _____

Email: _____

How to pay:

1. **By telephone**: call the TBS order line on 01206 522 800 and quote OBBSHC. Phone lines are open between Monday – Friday, 8.30am – 5.30pm.

2. **By post**: send a cheque for the full amount payable to TBS Ltd. and send the form to:

   Freepost RLUL-SJGC-SGKJ,
   Cash Sales/Direct Mail Dept.,
   The Book Service,
   Colchester Road, Frating,
   Colchester CO7 7DW